LY

Simon Armitage

POET LAUREATE

faber

§

Are they the suburbs or is that the sea?
In a rusty two-seater we were flying
along the coast, the buildings below flowing
like waves, the roads now watery seams

and ranks of white horses,
the ocean all rows and lines,
all avenues, streets and lanes,
the light like sunburst on tiled houses

after rain. I thought how body and soul
might do-si-do, or mingle or curdle
in some no-man's-land slash grey area;

I saw an angel's smile
in the throat of a gargoyle,
heard tube trains under the great aria.

§

My soul said, 'I want driving lessons
and some high-end walking boots.
I wanna hit the road and go walkabout,
not wallow here in bedsores and friction lesions

watching you doing your dirty business
behind bedroom curtains, in the bath-
room, seeing you birth
your ickle sonnets. Jeeeesus.

Remember that big weekender,
the roller coaster, when your live-in lodger
floated free as the train cornered?

Or when we got front-ended
on the dodgems
and I was thrown forward . . .'

§

Under a moorland pylon we found a stash
of high-voltage insulators
stockpiled for installation at some later
date. Made of thick aquamarine glass

and hollow, like giant thimbles,
there was no argument
they'd make great ornaments,
being obvious symbols

of the disconnect between thought and feeling
and the see-through wall between here and heaven.
My soul wanted to take them,

but I said no. That would be stealing,
and in any case they were really heavy.
Then my soul wanted to break them.

§

My soul said, 'I'm my own life-force, man, not
some inner foetus
or one of those baby scan photos
pinned with a fridge magnet.

Your trouble is
you don't know your qualia
from your koalas,
your watchamacallits from your thingummyjigs.

Meet me halfway.
Look for me in the interstices
between the wheelie bins, in the sketchy margin

where arm-wrestle meets handshake,
in the motorway services
between Pule Hill and Wednesday morning.'

§

I carried a glass shower door
out of a top-storey flat, but as I stepped
onto the balcony I stubbed
the bottom corner on the stone floor.

In that instant of whip-crack violence
the pane detonated and the gods stared
at the hole in the world and I stood
in a glittering porridge of false diamonds.

A wisp of white powder ghosted
between the quaint parallels
of an English Manhattan,

and my outstretched arms hosted
a sudden nothing. This is a parable
but it also happened.

§

My soul said, 'Obviously I'm a barn owl:
the ghost onesie, the heart-shaped face.
And I'm the Northern Lights, I'm High Force
and the earthy breath of essential balms and oils.

Naturally I'm a firefly, an albino narwhal,
a double rainbow, the lone curlew
patrolling the dawn curfew,
the pearl in the oyster blah blah blah.

True. But I'm also
the last car in the car park,
the blue smoke over the crash site,

the outskirts of Oslo.
The tangled knot in the parachute pack.
The taste of creosote.'

§

There was a steep grass bank then a field
stubbled with bull rushes, bearded with vetch,
then a ditch
and a thin stream that a child could ford

in one stride. Then a red brick wall,
built in plain and simple
'stretcher' style, about six feet long, single
skin, maximum five courses tall.

It kept nothing in, nothing out, offered
no shelter or shade, but that's where
the snow started

to fall cinematically upward,
and a figure balanced there
on the low red wall, unseen and stared at.

§

My soul said, 'What if *you're* the soul
and *I'm* the body?
How does that feel, buddy?'
I said, 'Like the lone leopard seal

in Gweek seal sanctuary
doing lengths and circuits.
Like a shabby brown bear in the last dirty old circus
dancing to Las Ketchup. And actually

I get why you're always bellyaching,
having to clown and cavort
in tight circumferences,

tethered to a spine. Backbreaking.
Would I be happy having to cringe and contort
that way? Under no circumstances.'

§

I suspect my soul is unfaithful,
two-timing me, creeping
around in the small hours, sneaking
about. One word: *ungrateful.*

'I'm just bored out of my tree, and lonely,'
my soul said. 'At night when you're cataleptic
I'm mainlining any old illumination into my optic
nerve. Sometimes I'm the only

soul at the empty intersection,
gawping at narcoleptic traffic lights.
Or I'm mooching

like a lost child at the petrol station,
infantilised
by the glittering shrine of the cash machine.'

§

My soul tells me the best coins aren't magnetic.
It's hardly nuclear science
or arcane knowledge gleaned at a seance
through the *black curtain*. He's being enigmatic,

saying he has *worth*
and won't be lured or fished
out of his lair, won't be flushed
from his purse. He's saying he's *wealth*.

'Did you ever sleep in a van
in winter?' he says. 'Every breath cast
as an ice sculpture, the night tasting of metal,

like sleeping in a tin can.
But the cops go bulleting past,
sirens truffling for worthless medals.'

§

Soul, some believe the mind is your mansion,
or you live in the breath.
Others say in the length, width and breadth
of the human frame you have no physical dimension.

Some say you snooze in the body's hammock
while the body's wide awake,
but while the body slumbers you make
havoc.

Personally I reckon you're quite
something, hitching through dark matter
and clear blue ether,

ducking and diving between quarks,
leapfrogging atom to atom.
Not being here but not being elsewhere either.

§

What if my soul has a soul of its own?
Some closet homunculus
hunkered down in its subconscious,
squatting in *my* bones.

And what if that stowaway soul
has its own soul as well, souls within
souls within souls, all churning and writhing
inside their cells,

all blessed or cursed with creases
and kinks: this one's a member of Mensa,
this one cuts itself, this one stutters,

this one sells state secrets?
'Or what if you have no soul whatsoever?'
one of my souls mutters.

§

'Master builders of ancient castles
and steeples
inserted brittle glass needles
between the colossal

stone blocks, so if the structures
moved by a hair's breadth
or even one Planck length
the glass would fracture.

None of this is strictly accurate,'
my soul said, 'but you get the drift.
The moment things go pear-shaped

I'm on the first helicopter out.
The millisecond things start to shift
I'll know, my Great Pyramid, my Empire State.'

§

My soul said, 'I guess I was lucky
being assigned to a la-di-da laureate.
I could have ended up in a laundrette
or call centre, I could have been a lackey

or gofer for some total vanilla.
Sure, it was boring watching Mr Scrabble
scratch and scribble
his precious sestinas and villanelles,

but I got to visit some fancy places,
and eavesdropped a thing or two
among thrones and crowns.

What did she say that time at the Palace:
"I think it's marvellous what you do,
seeing things and writing them down."'

§

My soul says, 'Happy birthday, Simon.'
I'm waiting for some snide
remark, the sarky comment from the side
of the mouth, but he's silent.

I put on my old boots and hike
up Old Mount Road, around Pule Hill,
then go for a long old haul
on my old mountain bike.

He's slumped in the inglenook
when I get home. 'When you were small
I gave you a party balloon,' he whispers.

'But like a witless nincompoop
you let it go; I remember your gormless smile
as it sailed off into non-existence.'

First published in 2023
in a signed limited edition
by Faber & Faber Ltd
The Bindery
51 Hatton Garden
London ec1n 8hn

Typeset by Hamish Ironside
Printed in the UK by TJ Books Ltd, Padstow, Cornwall

A CIP record for this book is available from the British Library

isbn 978-0-571-38635-2

FSC
www.fsc.org
MIX
Paper from
responsible sources
FSC® C013056